# HEAD-to-HEAD

## By Jake Black

SCHOLASTIC

an imprint of
**SCHOLASTIC**
www.scholastic.com

Copyright © 2012 becker&mayer! LLC

Published by Tangerine Press, an imprint of Scholastic Inc.,
557 Broadway, New York, NY 10012
Scholastic Canada Ltd., Markham, Ontario

becker&mayer!
BOOK PRODUCERS

*WWE Head-to-Head* is produced by becker&mayer! LLC
11120 NE 33rd Place, Suite 101
Bellevue, WA 98004

www.beckermayer.com

Scholastic and Tangerine Press and associated logos are trademarks and/or registered trademarks of Scholastic Inc.

All rights reserved.

No part of this book may be reproduced, stored in a retrieval system, or transmitted in any form or by any means,
electronic, mechanical, photocopying, recording, or otherwise, without the prior permission of Tangerine Press.

All WWE programming, talent names, images, likenesses, slogans, wrestling moves, trademarks, logos and copyrights are the exclusive
property of WWE and its subsidiaries. All other trademarks, logos and copyrights are the property of their respective owners.

© 2012 WWE. All Rights Reserved.

If you have questions or comments about this product, please visit www.beckermayer.com/customerservice and
click on Customer Service Request Form.

Written by Jake Black
Edited by Betsy Henry Pringle
Designed by Rosanna Brockley
Production management by Jennifer Marx
Photo research by Katie del Rosario
Design assistance by Ryan Hobson

TP4238-1  10/11
Printed in the United States of America
10 9 8 7 6 5 4 3 2 1
ISBN: 978-0-545-42952-8

11844

# HEAD-TO-HEAD

The greatest Superstars and Divas of *SmackDown* and *Raw* are stepping into the ring to prove—once and for all—who is the most dominant competitor in the WWE. For each head-to-head match, you'll get the stats and facts you need to pick a winner. On page 64, discover whom the experts chose—and how the plays went down.

## THE MATCHUPS

# JOHN CENA vs. CM PUNK

John Cena is known as the face of WWE. You'll find his image on the covers of magazines, collectible cups, and more. Superstar CM Punk wants what Cena has—to be the face of the company. Punk feels he is the best in the world, but Cena disagrees.

## John Cena

With catch phrases like "The champ is here," John Cena has boldly declared that he is WWE's top Superstar. He's made movies, appeared in numerous television shows, and become a star outside of the WWE. No matter what success he has outside of the ring, Cena maintains his true passion: being a WWE Superstar.

## INFO

| | |
|---|---|
| **Height** | 6'1" |
| **Weight** | 240 lbs. |
| **From** | West Newbury, Massachusetts |
| **Signature Move** | Attitude Adjustment; STF (Stepover Toehold Facelock) |
| **Career Highlights** | World Heavyweight Champion; WWE Champion; United States Champion; World Tag Team Champion; WWE Tag Team Champion; Royal Rumble Winner (2008) |

## STATS

| Intensity | Strength | Speed | Courage | Brains |
|---|---|---|---|---|
| 8 | 8 | 7 | 7 | 9 |

# THE SHOWDOWN:

Cena and Punk stare hard at each other from across the ring. Both Superstars have legions of fans cheering them on. Both are strong competitors, and each has an arsenal of moves. Both strike quickly and effectively, and both have held the WWE Championship. Even after hitting his opponent with everything he has, neither man dominates enough to pin the other for a three count.

## CM Punk

CM Punk doesn't drink alcohol, use drugs, or smoke. He lives the so-called straight edge lifestyle to keep his body in the best shape possible. He has impressive in-ring technical skills, as well. It's well known that CM Punk hates big corporations like the WWE. A rebel, he defies authority, doing whatever he wants whenever he wants.

## STATS

| Intensity | Strength | Speed | Courage | Brains |
|-----------|----------|-------|---------|--------|
| 7 | 7 | 7 | 9 | 8 |

## INFO

| | |
|---|---|
| 6'1" | Height |
| 222 lbs. | Weight |
| Chicago, Illinois | From |
| GTS (Go to Sleep); Anaconda Vise | Signature Move |
| WWE Champion; World Heavyweight Champion; ECW Champion; World Tag Team Champion; Intercontinental Champion | Career Highlights |

# UNDERTAKER vs. KANE

Few rivalries match the heat and intensity of the one between Undertaker and Kane. The two brothers have battled each other since they were children. Setting aside their family relationship, they have gone toe-to-toe for decades. And in doing so, each has called upon the powers of the dark side to help him win the battle.

## Undertaker

The man from the dark side, the Undertaker, has competed in the WWE for two decades. His legend surpasses nearly all other WWE Superstars. He's held countless championships and "buried" countless opponents. His fans, known as the "creatures of the night," cheer him on in every encounter. Perhaps, Undertaker's best accomplishment is his WrestleMania winning streak. For 19 years, he's been undefeated at WWE's biggest event. Can anyone stop him?

## INFO

| | |
|---|---|
| Height | 6'10" |
| Weight | 299 lbs. |
| From | Death Valley |
| Signature Move | Chokeslam; Tombstone; Last Ride |
| Career Highlights | WWE Champion; World Heavyweight Champion; World Tag Team Champion; WCW Tag Team Champion; Hardcore Champion; WrestleMania Undefeated Streak (19-0) |

## STATS

| Intensity | Strength | Speed | Courage | Brains |
|---|---|---|---|---|
| 9 | 7 | 6 | 7 | 10 |

# THE SHOWDOWN:

Undertaker and Kane have been called the "Brothers of Destruction" because their matches get so personal and so dangerous—no one is safe. They've battled in massive cages, in graveyards, and even surrounded by fire. As the siblings charge toward each other, a massive explosion ensues. They exchange punches, hitting hard, but neither man backs down.

## Kane

The "Big Red Monster" has been a dominant force in the WWE for nearly fifteen years. In that time he has destroyed his opponents and put fear in the hearts of the WWE Universe. His incredible size and ability in the ring make him an almost unbeatable opponent. Few Superstars have been able to defeat Kane. His fiery intensity is too much for them to handle.

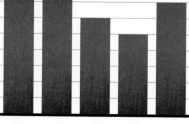

## STATS

| Intensity | Strength | Speed | Courage | Brains |
|-----------|----------|-------|---------|--------|
| 8 | 8 | 6 | 5 | 7 |

## INFO

| | |
|---|---|
| 7'0" | Height |
| 323 lbs. | Weight |
| Parts Unknown | From |
| Chokeslams | Signature Move |
| WWE Champion; World Heavyweight Champion; ECW Champion; Intercontinental Champion; World Tag Team Champion; WCW Tag Team Champion; Hardcore Champion | Career Highlights |

# MARK HENRY vs. BIG SHOW

The World's Strongest Man versus the World's Largest Athlete. It's a match for the ages! When two giants of immeasurable strength collide in the ring, it's as epic as the mythic legends of ancient times. Together, these Goliaths weigh nearly a half-ton. That's a lot of humanity to try to topple in the ring.

## Mark Henry

Competing around the world in international weightlifting competitions (including the Olympics), Mark Henry proved time and again that he was the strongest man on the planet. His strength, combined with a nasty mean streak, makes him a terrifying WWE Superstar.

| INFO | |
|---|---|
| Height | 6'4" |
| Weight | 398 lbs. |
| From | Silsbee, Texas |
| Signature Move | World's Strongest Slam |
| Career Highlights | ECW Champion; European Champion |

**STATS**

| Intensity | Strength | Speed | Courage | Brains |
|---|---|---|---|---|
| 7 | 10 | 4 | 5 | 6 |

# THE SHOWDOWN:

Both Mark Henry and Big Show are determined to hold the title as WWE's best giant. To achieve this, each must get past the other. This is no easy feat. Henry's stronger than anyone in the world. Big Show's bigger than every other athlete competing in any sport. May the best giant win.

## Big Show

No one is larger than the Big Show. And no one competes harder in the WWE ring. With his devastating chokeslam and a powerful right fist, Big Show has been at the top of the WWE mountain on numerous occasions. It's not surprising, since he is just about the size of a mountain! And few Superstars are strong enough to move such a mountain.

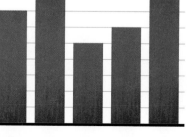

| | | | | |
|---|---|---|---|---|
| 7 | 8 | 5 | 6 | 8 |
| Intensity | Strength | Speed | Courage | Brains |

**STATS**

**INFO**

| | |
|---|---|
| 7'0" | Height |
| 485 lbs. | Weight |
| Tampa, Florida | From |
| Chokeslam; Knockout Punch; Colossal Clutch | Signature Move |
| ECW World Champion; WWE Champion; WCW Champion; World Tag Team Champion; WWE Hardcore Champion; United States Champion; WWE Tag Team Champion | Career Highlights |

# RANDY ORTON vs. CHRISTIAN

The World Heavyweight Championship, which has been around since the early 1900s, is the oldest title in sports entertainment history. To Randy Orton and Christian, it is the most important achievement in the world. Both Randy and Christian are obsessed with being the World Champion. The only thing each man must do to win the title is beat the other Superstar.

## Randy Orton

A third generation WWE Superstar, Randy Orton grew up knowing what it takes to be a winner in the ring. Known as "The Viper," Orton can strike at any time. He is extremely dangerous to his opponents and will stop at nothing to win his matches.

## INFO

| | |
|---|---|
| Height | 6'4" |
| Weight | 245 lbs. |
| From | St. Louis, Missouri |
| Signature Move | RKO |
| Career Highlights | WWE Champion; World Heavyweight Champion; Intercontinental Champion; World Tag Team Champion; Royal Rumble Winner (2009) |

## STATS

| Intensity | Strength | Speed | Courage | Brains |
|---|---|---|---|---|
| 8 | 5 | 6 | 7 | 7 |

# THE SHOWDOWN:

Armed with similar size, speed, and strength, Randy Orton and Christian are about as evenly matched in the ring as any two Superstars can be. Their battles go down to the wire, and it's nearly impossible to predict the winner. Will Orton hit his patented RKO—or will Christian sneak a surprise Killswitch? The two combatants lock up shoulder to arm, until Randy Orton forces Christian hard into the corner.

## Christian

Christian began his WWE tenure with his best friend, WWE Legend Edge. The two made up one of the most popular tag teams in history. Once on his own, though, Christian slowly became obsessed with winning the World Heavyweight Championship. He would do anything to capture the gold—even cheat.

### STATS

| 7 | 6 | 8 | 8 | 6 |
|---|---|---|---|---|
| Intensity | Strength | Speed | Courage | Brains |

### INFO

| | |
|---|---|
| 6'2" | Height |
| 227 lbs. | Weight |
| Toronto, Ontario, Canada | From |
| Killswitch | Signature Move |
| World Heavyweight Champion; ECW Champion; Intercontinental Champion; World Tag Team Champion; Light Heavyweight Champion; Hardcore Champion; European Champion | Career Highlights |

11

# THE MIZ vs. ALEX RILEY

Some of the greatest battles in history have been between a mentor and his protégé. This is the case with The Miz and Alex Riley. The Miz was A-Ry's mentor and pro on the second season of *WWE NXT*. The Miz then hired Alex Riley as his personal assistant. The two were inseparable for a long time.

## The Miz

After taking the world of reality television by storm, The Miz entered the WWE, where he became the most "must see WWE Champion of all time." Miz carried the WWE Championship title with him everywhere he went, including to numerous television and media appearances. One thing's for sure: Miz Madness is everywhere!

## INFO

| | |
|---|---|
| Height | 6'1" |
| Weight | 231 lbs. |
| From | Cleveland, Ohio |
| Signature Move | Skull-Crushing Finale |
| Career Highlights | WWE Champion; WWE Tag Team Champion; World Tag Team Champion; United States Champion; Raw Money in the Bank Winner (2010) |

## STATS

| | | | | |
|---|---|---|---|---|
| 6 | 6 | 7 | 7 | 5 |
| Intensity | Strength | Speed | Courage | Brains |

# THE SHOWDOWN:

No one knows The Miz as well as Alex Riley does. After being his assistant for nearly a year, Riley understood all of The Miz's strengths and weaknesses. Once Miz fired Riley, the two battled frequently in the ring. Miz taught Riley a lot, but he didn't give away all his secrets. Riley doesn't waste any time—he charges the ring, nailing Miz with a mega clothesline.

## Alex Riley

Known as A-Ry, Alex Riley has finally broken out of his mentor's shadow. Extremely talented in the ring, Riley is an up-and-coming Superstar in the WWE. He already holds several victories over his former teacher and has set his sights on dominating the entire WWE.

| 6 | 7 | 7 | 5 | 6 |
|---|---|---|---|---|
| Intensity | Strength | Speed | Courage | Brains |

**STATS**

| | |
|---|---|
| 6'2" | Height |
| 251 lbs. | Weight |
| Washington, D.C. | From |
| DDT | Signature Move |
| Mentored by The Miz on WWE NXT | Career Highlights |

**INFO**

# JOHN MORRISON vs. R-TRUTH

Former friends—now bitter enemies—John Morrison and R-Truth have a heated rivalry that has thrilled the WWE Universe time and again. The former tag team partners can no longer stand to be around each other, except inside the ring. Even then, each man tries to win quickly so he can get away from his former friend.

## John Morrison

John Morrison is used to living the fast-paced life of a Hollywood star. He can always be seen at the coolest parties, with the biggest celebrities. But don't let that fool you. He's a tough competitor in the ring and has won the championships to prove it.

## INFO

| | |
|---|---|
| Height | 6'1" |
| Weight | 224 lbs. |
| From | Los Angeles, California |
| Signature Move | Starship Pain; The Moonlight Drive |
| Career Highlights | Intercontinental Champion; ECW Champion; WWE Tag Team Champion |

## STATS

| Intensity | Strength | Speed | Courage | Brains |
|---|---|---|---|---|
| 6 | 6 | 8 | 7 | 8 |

# THE SHOWDOWN:

R-Truth is a street tough Superstar who has no problem competing against anyone in the ring. John Morrison is a high flyer whose smooth style is exciting to watch. When these two different approaches to in-ring competition clash, they explode in a great match. But John Morrison had better watch his back—R-Truth has no problem using dirty tricks, such as hitting his opponent from behind, to gain an early advantage.

## R-Truth

R-Truth believes that he's been kept out of the top spots in the WWE by a conspiracy led by the top WWE officials and supported by the WWE Universe. His complaints about all the "Little Jimmies" of the WWE Universe keeping him down have made him one of the most hated WWE Superstars in recent memory.

| | | | | |
|---|---|---|---|---|
| 7 | 7 | 7 | 4 | 6 |
| Intensity | Strength | Speed | Courage | Brains |

**STATS**

| | |
|---|---|
| 6'2" | Height |
| 235 lbs. | Weight |
| Charlotte, North Carolina | From |
| Lie Detector | Signature Move |
| United States Champion | Career Highlights |

**INFO**

# DOLPH ZIGGLER vs. KOFI KINGSTON

What began as two WWE Superstars striving to win a title has become personal. Dolph Ziggler and Kofi Kingston have had a series of matches—trading victories back and forth, and exciting the WWE Universe. The pair of Superstars have similar in-ring styles, though Ziggler is more of a grappler, while Kofi likes flying.

## Dolph Ziggler

Dolph Ziggler claims to be "perfection." He boasts that he has the greatest body ever seen in sports entertainment. He also has Vickie Guerrero at his side. Dolph provides the brawn, and Vickie is the brain. Together, they are unstoppable, capturing titles and winning matches.

## INFO

| | |
|---|---|
| Height | 6'0" |
| Weight | 223 lbs. |
| From | Hollywood, Florida |
| Signature Move | The Zig Zag |
| Career Highlights | World Heavyweight Champion; Intercontinental Champion; United States Champion |

## STATS

| Intensity | Strength | Speed | Courage | Brains |
|---|---|---|---|---|
| 6 | 6 | 7 | 4 | 5 |

16

# THE SHOWDOWN:

Kofi Kingston is more popular than Dolph Ziggler, and he has the fan support to back him up. But don't underestimate the influence that Dolph Ziggler's "business associate" Vickie Guerrero can have on the match's outcome. She motivates Ziggler, and even attacks Kofi when the referee isn't looking.

## Kofi Kingston

Energetic, happy, and exciting, Kofi Kingston has taken the WWE Universe by storm. He has an easy-going demeanor, unless he is unfairly attacked by his opponents. Then, watch out! Kofi will strike back from the air with his trademark "Boom, Boom, Boom" offense.

### STATS

| 5 | 6 | 9 | 7 | 8 |
|---|---|---|---|---|
| Intensity | Strength | Speed | Courage | Brains |

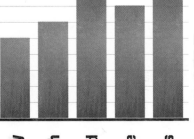

### INFO

| | |
|---|---|
| 6'1" | Height |
| 221 lbs. | Weight |
| Ghana, West Africa | From |
| Trouble in Paradise | Signature Move |
| Intercontinental Champion; World Tag Team Champion; United States Champion | Career Highlights |

# REY MYSTERIO vs. ALBERTO DEL RIO

Alberto Del Rio likes the finer things in life. Rey Mysterio is a hardworking husband and father. Alberto Del Rio uses submission holds to win matches. Rey Mysterio soars through the air to defeat his opponents. Alberto Del Rio can't stand the fans in the WWE Universe. Rey Mysterio depends on the WWE Universe to motivate him.

## Rey Mysterio

Since bursting onto the sports entertainment scene in the 1990s, Rey Mysterio has captured the imaginations of WWE fans the world over. The proud Latino wears a mask to celebrate his heritage. With his wide-range aerial moves, Rey is thrilling to watch in the ring.

## INFO

| | |
|---|---|
| Height | 5'6" |
| Weight | 175 lbs. |
| From | San Diego, California |
| Signature Move | 619; West Coast Pop |
| Career Highlights | WWE Champion; World Heavyweight Champion; Royal Rumble Winner (2006); Cruiserweight Champion; WWE Tag Team Champion; WCW Tag Team Champion; Intercontinental Champion |

## STATS

| Intensity | Strength | Speed | Courage | Brains |
|---|---|---|---|---|
| 6 | 7 | 9 | 6 | 8 |

# THE SHOWDOWN:

Two Latino Superstars; two very different lifestyles. Everything about Rey Mysterio and Alberto Del Rio is different. However, they are both the very best at what they do. Both Superstars are determined, and both are passionate about sports entertainment. Del Rio might be a bigger man physically, but Rey's love for his family and the WWE fans makes him a bigger man in other ways. Rey begins the match by springing off the ropes and tackling Del Rio.

## Alberto Del Rio

Alberto Del Rio is the greatest man to ever grace WWE with his presence—just ask him. Riding to the ring in expensive cars and having his own personal ring announcer, Del Rio flaunts his wealth and power. But money can't buy victories in the ring. Fortunately, Del Rio has the skills necessary to earn those, too.

## STATS

| | | | | |
|---|---|---|---|---|
| 4 | 6 | 7 | 8 | 7 |
| Intensity | Strength | Speed | Courage | Brains |

## INFO

| | |
|---|---|
| 6'5" | Height |
| 263 lbs. | Weight |
| San Luis Potosi, Mexico | From |
| Cross Armbreaker | Signature Move |
| Royal Rumble Winner (2011); Raw Money in the Bank Winner (2011); WWE Champion | Career Highlights |

# MICHAEL MCGILLICUTTY vs. SANTINO MARELLA

Michael McGillicutty and Santino Marella are not strangers to each other. They have squared off in the squared circle several times as members of opposing tag teams, usually battling over the WWE Tag Team Championship. McGillicutty's focused intensity and Santino's goofy attitude often make for entertaining encounters.

## Michael McGillicutty

Michael McGillicutty has great technique and an even better heritage behind him every time he enters the ring. The son of WWE Hall of Famer "Mr. Perfect" Curt Hennig, the former Nexus member is a formidable adversary for any WWE Superstar.

## INFO

| | |
|---|---|
| Height | 6'3" |
| Weight | 232 lbs. |
| From | Champlin, Minnesota |
| Signature Move | McGillicutter |
| Career Highlights | WE Tag Team Champion; Son of WWE Hall of Famer "Mr. Perfect" Curt Hennig; Former member of Nexus; Mentored by Kofi Kingston on WWE NXT |

## STATS

| Intensity | Strength | Speed | Courage | Brains |
|---|---|---|---|---|
| 6 | 8 | 8 | 6 | 6 |

# THE SHOWDOWN:

When facing each other one-on-one—as opposed to being part of a tag team—McGillicutty and Marella are forced to throw everything they have into the match. A strong technical background gives McGillicutty an edge, while Marella relies more on luck and timing. Because of their different wrestling styles, the advantage goes to McGillicutty, who puts hold after hold on Marella.

## Santino Marella

Santino Marella's entrance to the WWE came as a fluke. He was picked out of the audience to compete for the Intercontinental Championship during a WWE event in his home country of Italy. Little did the WWE realize that it was seeing the birth of a new WWE Superstar. With his trademark unibrow and "terrifying" Cobra Strike, Santino is beloved by the WWE Universe.

## STATS

| 3 | 5 | 6 | 4 | 4 |
|---|---|---|---|---|
| Intensity | Strength | Speed | Courage | Brains |

## INFO

| | |
|---|---|
| 5'10" | Height |
| 227 lbs. | Weight |
| Calabria, Italy | From |
| The Cobra | Signature Move |
| Intercontinental Champion; WWE Tag Team Champion | Career Highlights |

# YOSHI TATSU VS. TYSON KIDD

Tradition plays an important role in the lives of both Yoshi Tatsu and Tyson Kidd. Tatsu is proud to carry on the legacy of great Japanese Superstars like Hall of Famer Antonio Inoki. Tyson Kidd is the last graduate of the legendary Hart Dungeon, carrying on the tradition of all-time greats like Bret "Hit Man" Hart and the "British Bulldog" Davey Boy Smith.

## Yoshi Tatsu

Yoshi Tatsu has a colorful and entertaining persona. He loves techno music and is proud of his Japanese heritage and culture. Sports entertainment is extremely popular in Japan, and Yoshi Tatsu is just as famous there. The WWE Universe loves watching his matches, but don't blink or you might miss something amazing!

## INFO

| | |
|---|---|
| Height | 6'1" |
| Weight | 220 lbs. |
| From | Tokyo, Japan |
| Signature Move | Yoshi Kick |
| Career Highlights | Mentor to Byron Saxton on WWE NXT |

## STATS

| Intensity | Strength | Speed | Courage | Brains |
|---|---|---|---|---|
| 3 | 4 | 8 | 5 | 6 |

# THE SHOWDOWN:

Both Tyson and Yoshi are super fast. With lightning quick moves and brilliant technical prowess, the two can go hold-for-hold with each other. Tyson is more aggressive, but Yoshi is a little faster. The two international sensations make the perfect opponents.

## Tyson Kidd

Growing up in Alberta, Canada, Tyson Kidd spent his childhood hanging out with the legendary wrestlers in the Hart family. The Harts were known for their phenomenal technical ability, which they passed along to Tyson. He learned the ins and outs of wrestling in the basement, known as the Dungeon, of the Hart home.

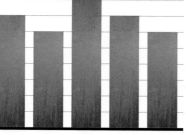

| 7 | 6 | 9 | 7 | 6 |
|---|---|---|---|---|
| Intensity | Strength | Speed | Courage | Brains |

**STATS**

| | |
|---|---|
| 5'10" | **Height** |
| 199 lbs. | **Weight** |
| Calgary, Alberta, Canada | **From** |
| Sharpshooter | **Signature Move** |
| Unified Tag Team Champion; WWE Tag Team Champion; Trained by WWE Hall of Famer Bret Hart; Last Graduate of the Infamous Hart Dungeon | **Career Highlights** |

**INFO**

# ZACK RYDER VS. CURT HAWKINS

Zack Ryder and Curt Hawkins were, at one time, the best of friends. They were loyal minions of WWE Legend Edge. Called the Edge-Heads, Ryder and Hawkins traveled the world together, doing Edge's bidding. With Edge out of the picture, though, the two no longer need each other and they go their separate ways.

## Zack Ryder

To say that Zack Ryder is an Internet sensation is putting it mildly. The brightly clad Superstar has millions of people watching his escapades online and calling for him to appear on TV more often. The "Ryder Revolution" has gone viral, and catapulted "Mr. Woo-Woo-Woo" to the top of the WWE.

| INFO | |
|---|---|
| Height | 6'1" |
| Weight | 214 lbs. |
| From | Long Island, New York |
| Signature Move | Zack Attack; Rough Ryder |
| Career Highlights | WWE Tag Team Champion |

### STATS

| Intensity | Strength | Speed | Courage | Brains |
|---|---|---|---|---|
| 4 | 7 | 7 | 5 | 6 |

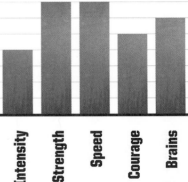

# THE SHOWDOWN:

Ryder and Hawkins are about as evenly matched as two people can be. They are nearly identical in size, speed, and skill. If either man has an advantage, it might be Ryder. He has amassed a large following in the WWE Universe, and the fans have been known to motivate him to victory. The bell rings, the crowd cheers Ryder, and he slams Hawkins with a fast cross-body press.

## Curt Hawkins

Curt Hawkins rose to prominence during his time as an Edge-Head. Since breaking off from Edge, Hawkins has been a force to be reckoned with on *Friday Night SmackDown*. He quietly waits for the best opportunity to strike his opponent, something he learned from Edge, the "ultimate opportunist."

| 4 | 6 | 7 | 5 | 5 |
|---|---|---|---|---|

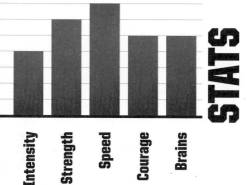

**STATS**

Intensity · Strength · Speed · Courage · Brains

| | |
|---|---|
| 6'1" | **Height** |
| 221 lbs. | **Weight** |
| Queens, New York | **From** |
| Heat-Seeking Elbow | **Signature Move** |
| WWE Tag Team Champion | **Career Highlights** |

**INFO**

# TRIPLE H vs. "STONE COLD" STEVE AUSTIN

These are arguably the two greatest Superstars in WWE history. Although they have a long historic rivalry, their paths have not crossed recently. Nevertheless, a match between Triple H and Steve Austin is every fan's dream. Both hold multiple WWE Championships. Both have incredible in-ring ability. And both are megastars.

## Triple H

Triple H is known by many nicknames, including "The Game," "The King of Kings," and the "Cerebral Assassin." He represents the pinnacle of WWE Superstardom. He's done it all in WWE. Triple H has been a champion, an authority figure, and even the son-in-law of WWE founder and former chairman Vince McMahon.

### INFO

| | |
|---|---|
| Height | 6'4" |
| Weight | 255 lbs. |
| From | Greenwich, Connecticut |
| Signature Move | Pedigree |
| Career Highlights | WWE Champion; World Heavyweight Champion; Intercontinental Champion; Unified WWE Tag Team Champion; World Tag Team Champion; European Champion; King of the Ring (1997); Royal Rumble Winner (2002) |

### STATS

| Intensity | Strength | Speed | Courage | Brains |
|---|---|---|---|---|
| 9 | 9 | 8 | 9 | 9 |

# THE SHOWDOWN:

Neither Triple H nor "Stone Cold" Steve Austin will run from a fight. In fact, they are both likely to run *toward* one. The intensity of this confrontation is off the charts. "The Game" and "Stone Cold" exchange blows and holds, and the fans of the WWE Universe who came to see two legendary titans battle toe-to-toe are the real winners.

## "Stone Cold" Steve Austin

In the 1990s, "Stone Cold" Steve Austin carried the WWE to the highest highs it would ever reach. His rivalry with the Chairman Vince McMahon was legendary. This tough brawler represented the common man— and was beloved by him, too. With numerous accolades under his belt, Austin was a shoo-in for induction into the WWE Hall of Fame.

| 9 | 9 | 7 | 8 | 9 | |
|---|---|---|---|---|---|
| Intensity | Strength | Speed | Courage | Brains | **STATS** |

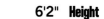

| | |
|---|---|
| 6'2" | **Height** |
| 252 lbs. | **Weight** |
| Victoria, Texas | **From** |
| Stone Cold Stunner | **Signature Move** |
| WWE Champion; Intercontinental Champion; World Tag Team Champion; King of the Ring (1996); Royal Rumble winner (1997, 1998, 2001); United States Champion; WCW Tag Team Champion; WWE Hall of Fame | **Career Highlights** |

**INFO**

# BRODUS CLAY vs. JOHNNY CURTIS

A pair of up-and-coming Superstars in the WWE, Brodus Clay and Johnny Curtis are desperate to make their marks. These hungry young lions are ready to climb the ladder of success, rung by rung, to reach the WWE Championship. They may be starting at the bottom, but neither of these brawlers will be there for long.

## Brodus Clay

Beginning as a rookie on *WWE NXT*, Brodus Clay impressed the WWE Universe with his ruthless aggression. He also impressed Alberto Del Rio, who hired Brodus to be his bodyguard for a time on *Friday Night SmackDown*. No longer responsible for Del Rio's safety, Brodus Clay can focus on his own career and aspirations.

## INFO

| | |
|---|---|
| Height | 6'8" |
| Weight | 367 lbs. |
| From | Pasadena, California |
| Signature Move | Running Splash |
| Career Highlights | Mentored by Ted DiBiase and Maryse on WWE NXT |

## STATS

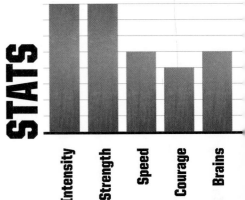

| Intensity | Strength | Speed | Courage | Brains |
|---|---|---|---|---|
| 8 | 8 | 5 | 4 | 5 |

# THE SHOWDOWN:

To get to the top of the WWE, Brodus and Johnny will have to get past each other. Brodus's strength and cold, menacing attitude give him an advantage. But Johnny's clever mind might help him overcome Brodus. It's a classic tale of brains versus brawn. Brodus reaches to grab Johnny in a bear hug, but Johnny avoids, pointing to his brain in the process.

## Johnny Curtis

Johnny Curtis has a silly personality. Known for his quick-witted puns, he has made the fans in the WWE Universe laugh time and again. He also has good ability in the ring. Since moving from *WWE NXT* to *Friday Night SmackDown*, Johnny has proved that he's smart. Those smarts let him make his puns, but they have occasionally earned him the anger of the other WWE Superstars.

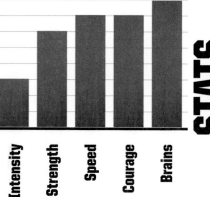

| | 3 | 6 | 7 | 7 | 8 |
|---|---|---|---|---|---|
| **STATS** | Intensity | Strength | Speed | Courage | Brains |

| | |
|---|---|
| 6'3" | **Height** |
| 240 lbs. | **Weight** |
| Westbrook, Maine | **From** |
| Maine Jam | **Signature Move** |
| Mentored by R-Truth on WWE NXT | **Career Highlights** |

**INFO**

# MASON RYAN vs. DAVID OTUNGA

Mason Ryan and David Otunga are both former members of the Nexus, but now they can't stand each other. Each brawler believes he was the top man in the Nexus and deserves a better spot in the WWE.

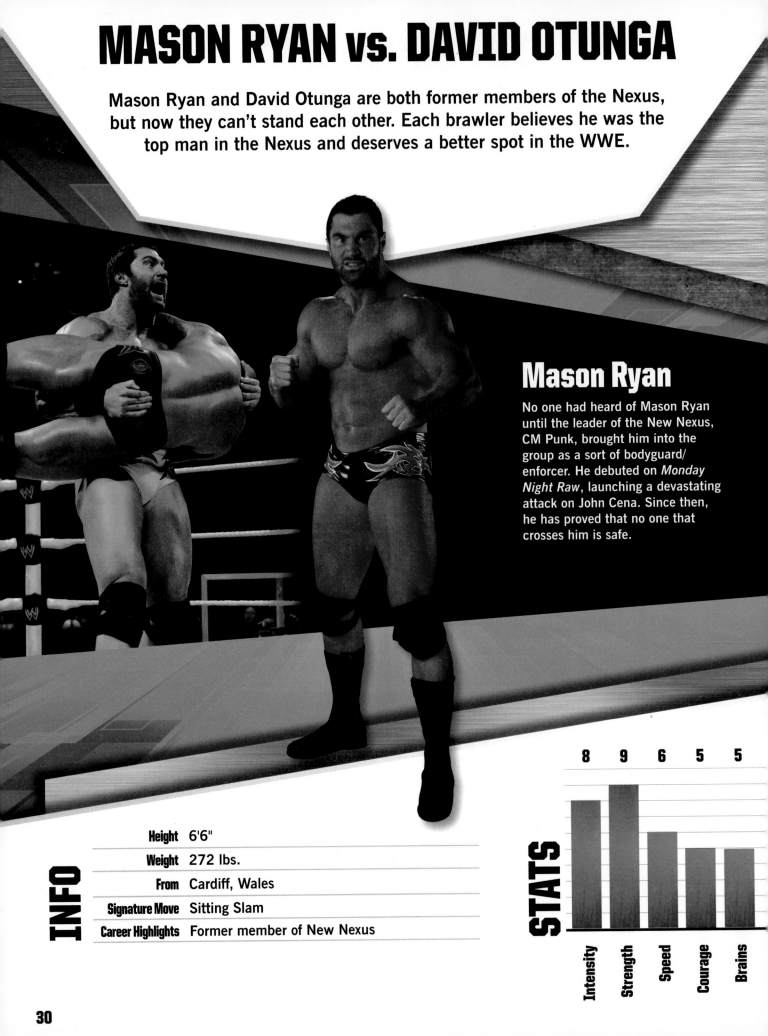

## Mason Ryan

No one had heard of Mason Ryan until the leader of the New Nexus, CM Punk, brought him into the group as a sort of bodyguard/enforcer. He debuted on *Monday Night Raw*, launching a devastating attack on John Cena. Since then, he has proved that no one that crosses him is safe.

### INFO

| | |
|---|---|
| Height | 6'6" |
| Weight | 272 lbs. |
| From | Cardiff, Wales |
| Signature Move | Sitting Slam |
| Career Highlights | Former member of New Nexus |

### STATS

| Intensity | Strength | Speed | Courage | Brains |
|---|---|---|---|---|
| 8 | 9 | 6 | 5 | 5 |

# THE SHOWDOWN:

Both Otunga and Ryan are extremely powerful, and their collision in the ring is like two giant rams locking horns in a life-or-death struggle. Ryan gets off to the early lead with a big power slam, but Otunga lashes back with a slam of his own.

## David Otunga

As an original member of Nexus, David Otunga had an army of Superstars by his side when he walked into the ring. Since the end of Nexus, David's been on his own. He doesn't have a problem with that, though. In the ring, he's a powerful competitor who hates to lose.

| | | | | |
|---|---|---|---|---|
| 7 | 8 | 5 | 6 | 5 |
| Intensity | Strength | Speed | Courage | Brains |

**STATS**

| | |
|---|---|
| 6'0" | Height |
| 250 lbs. | Weight |
| Hollywood, California | From |
| Spinebuster | Signature Move |
| WWE Tag Team Champion; Former member of Nexus | Career Highlights |

**INFO**

31

# JEY USO vs. JUSTIN GABRIEL

It's Samoa versus South Africa as one of the Uso twins, Jey, steps into the ring with South Africa's favorite son, Justin Gabriel. Jey has a slight size advantage on Gabriel, but Justin believes that it's not the size of the dog in the fight, but the size of the fight in the dog that matters.

## Jey Uso

Jey Uso and his twin brother, Jimmy, made a strong statement in their WWE debut by attacking the then-WWE Tag Team Champions, the Hart Dynasty. Since then, the Usos have made their reputation as being incredibly tough—especially Jey, who takes on all comers.

| INFO | |
|---|---|
| Height | 6'2" |
| Weight | 235 lbs. |
| From | San Francisco, California |
| Signature Move | Top Rope Splash |
| Career Highlights | Son of WWE Legend Rikishi |

## STATS

| Intensity | Strength | Speed | Courage | Brains |
|---|---|---|---|---|
| 7 | 6 | 7 | 6 | 6 |

# THE SHOWDOWN:

As these two fierce competitors face off against each other, the WWE Universe knows it will be an aerial display. Neither man starts by flying from the top rope, though. Justin runs toward Jey, but the strong Samoan nails him with a powerful dropkick.

## Justin Gabriel

Justin Gabriel used to think he needed to have his friends and allies around him to win matches. He was a member of Nexus and then The Corre before splitting from his friends and tag team partner to forge his own destiny. With a flashy style, Gabriel has thrilled the WWE Universe, amassing many wins in the process.

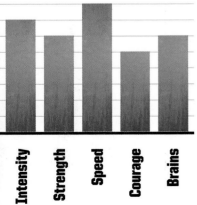

| | | |
|---|---|---|
| 7 | Intensity | |
| 6 | Strength | |
| 8 | Speed | |
| 5 | Courage | |
| 6 | Brains | |

**STATS**

| | |
|---|---|
| 6'1" | **Height** |
| 223 lbs. | **Weight** |
| Cape Town, South Africa | **From** |
| 450 Splash | **Signature Move** |
| WWE Tag Team Champion; Former member of Nexus and The Corre | **Career Highlights** |

**INFO**

# DANIEL BRYAN vs. CODY RHODES

Daniel Bryan is admired the world over for his technical ability in the ring, while Cody Rhodes was once admired for his dashing looks. Rhodes believes he lost his looks in a match, and now lashes out at the world. Daniel Bryan just wants to compete.

## Daniel Bryan

Daniel Bryan joined WWE as a rookie in the first season of *NXT*. A popular competitor in sports entertainment organizations in Japan and elsewhere, he had already established a strong fan base. Upon his arrival in WWE, his fans were excited to watch him ply his craft in the world's most watched company.

## INFO

| | |
|---|---|
| Height | 5'10" |
| Weight | 192 lbs. |
| From | Aberdeen, Washington |
| Signature Move | LeBell Lock |
| Career Highlights | United States Champion; SmackDown Money in the Bank Winner (2011); Trained by Shawn Michaels and William Regal |

## STATS

| Intensity | Strength | Speed | Courage | Brains |
|---|---|---|---|---|
| 5 | 7 | 7 | 7 | 7 |

# THE SHOWDOWN:

Cody Rhodes is so scared of having his beautiful face injured further that he wears a plastic mask in the ring. But the mask won't protect him from Daniel Bryan's technical moves. The two twist and turn, grappling and countering each other's holds in an amateur-style match.

## Cody Rhodes

The son of WWE Hall of Famer "The American Dream" Dusty Rhodes, Cody Rhodes has sports entertainment in his blood. His unique abilities in the ring have won him countless matches and set him on the path to follow in his father's footsteps. Although he believes he's been deformed because of his in-ring competition, Rhodes is a super threat to the WWE Superstars.

### STATS

| | Intensity | Strength | Speed | Courage | Brains |
|---|---|---|---|---|---|
| | 6 | 6 | 8 | 7 | 5 |

### INFO

| | |
|---|---|
| 6'1" | Height |
| 223 lbs. | Weight |
| Marietta, Georgia | From |
| Cross Rhodes | Signature Move |
| World Tag Team Championship; WWE Tag Team Championship; Son of WWE Hall of Famer "The American Dream" Dusty Rhodes; Intercontinental Champion | Career Highlights |

# HEATH SLATER vs. JIMMY USO

Heath Slater, the man known as the "One Man Rock Band," has everything to prove. Since abandoning The Corre, he's been a star on the rise. But Jimmy Uso, one half of the Uso brothers tag team, doesn't want Slater to succeed. In fact, Jimmy's main goal is to bring Heath down and steal his success, by any means necessary.

## Heath Slater

His fiery red hair flowing in the wind and his baby face good looks catching the attention of the WWE Universe, Heath Slater is making his own way in the WWE. No longer needing the help of his former teammates in Nexus and The Corre, Slater is ready to conquer the WWE and show everyone exactly why they call him the "One Man Rock Band."

## INFO

| | |
|---|---|
| Height | 6'2" |
| Weight | 232 lbs. |
| From | Pineville, West Virginia |
| Signature Move | Sweetness DDT |
| Career Highlights | WWE Tag Team Champion; Former member of Nexus and The Corre |

## STATS

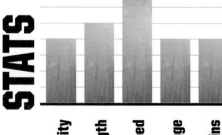

| Intensity | Strength | Speed | Courage | Brains |
|---|---|---|---|---|
| 4 | 5 | 7 | 4 | 4 |

# THE SHOWDOWN:

Slater and Uso share similar action-packed styles. When they collide in the ring, it's fast and furious. They run toward each other, smashing each other with a hard clothesline. Being so similar lets them jump to their feet simultaneously. Uso takes to the top rope, hoping to fly through the air and land on Slater. But Slater is ready to catch and slam his opponent to the ground.

## Jimmy Uso

Like his twin brother Jey, Jimmy Uso was raised to be a WWE Superstar from birth. His father, WWE legend Rikishi, taught Jimmy what it takes to compete in the ring. Jimmy also learned ancient Samoan war dances and is proud of his heritage—he's especially proud of what the Samoan people have brought to sports entertainment.

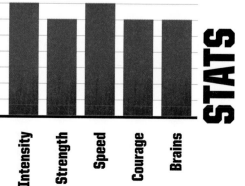

| | | | | |
|---|---|---|---|---|
| 7 | 6 | 7 | 6 | 6 |
| Intensity | Strength | Speed | Courage | Brains |

**STATS**

**INFO**

| | |
|---|---|
| 6'2" | Height |
| 240 lbs. | Weight |
| San Francisco, California | From |
| Samoan Drop | Signature Move |
| Son of WWE Legend Rikishi | Career Highlights |

# SHEAMUS vs. WADE BARRETT

Sheamus and Wade Barrett are angry. The two brawlers from the United Kingdom (Sheamus from Ireland and Barrett from England) feel that the WWE bosses have ignored their accomplishments. Neither man likes anyone else, and they both like to vent their anger and frustration in the ring.

## Sheamus

Sheamus astounded the WWE Universe by winning the Championship in his rookie year. He became famous for defeating John Cena in several matches, and for an intensity that overwhelmed his opponents. When he captured the 2010 King of the Ring, Sheamus sent a message to the WWE Universe: he was here to stay . . . and to dominate.

## INFO

| | |
|---|---|
| Height | 6'6" |
| Weight | 272 lbs. |
| From | Dublin, Ireland |
| Signature Move | High Cross; Brogue Kick; Irish Curse |
| Career Highlights | WWE Champion; United States Champion; King of the Ring (2010) |

## STATS

| Intensity | Strength | Speed | Courage | Brains |
|---|---|---|---|---|
| 8 | 8 | 6 | 7 | 7 |

# THE SHOWDOWN:

Barrett and Sheamus like to begin their matches in the same way—in the center of the ring, exchanging blows. They go back and forth, landing punches, chops, and elbows. Sheamus is the stronger of the two, so his blows land harder, but Barrett is driven to succeed and rarely feels any pain.

## Wade Barrett

Wade Barrett has accomplished a lot in a very short time. The winner of the first season of *WWE NXT*, Barrett went on to form both the Nexus and The Corre, groups of Superstars that dominated both *Monday Night Raw* and *Friday Night SmackDown*. Now on his own, Barrett has captured the Intercontinental Championship.

## STATS

| Intensity | Strength | Speed | Courage | Brains |
|-----------|----------|-------|---------|--------|
| 7 | 7 | 7 | 8 | 7 |

## INFO

| | |
|---|---|
| 6'5" | Height |
| 260 lbs. | Weight |
| Manchester, England | From |
| Wasteland Slam | Signature Move |
| NXT Winner (Season 1); Intercontinental Champion; Former leader of Nexus and The Corre | Career Highlights |

# EVAN BOURNE vs. JACK SWAGGER

Jack Swagger is not as happy as you'd think he would be. He's a former World Heavyweight Champion and a two-time All-American in amateur wrestling. But his efforts to get a WWE Championship match on *Monday Night Raw* have been cut short by Evan Bourne. Bourne has done everything he can to get under Swagger's skin.

## Evan Bourne

Evan Bourne has a big smile, and he flashes it every time he competes in the ring. His favorite thing to do is flip and fly around the ring, crushing opponents with super high dropkicks and his patented Air Bourne—a mid-air back flip splash that leaves his opponents and the WWE Universe breathless.

## INFO

| | |
|---|---|
| Height | 5'9" |
| Weight | 183 lbs. |
| From | St. Louis, Missouri |
| Signature Move | Air Bourne |
| Career Highlights | Slammy Award for "Best Finishing Move" (2008); WWE Tag Team Champion |

## STATS

| | | | | |
|---|---|---|---|---|
| 3 | 5 | 8 | 7 | 9 |
| Intensity | Strength | Speed | Courage | Brains |

# THE SHOWDOWN:

As Swagger and Bourne face off in the ring, Swagger has to do whatever is necessary to keep Bourne from climbing the ropes and using his arsenal of aerial moves. Swagger grabs Bourne as he tries climbing the ropes and quickly locks his arms around Bourne's ankle in an ankle lock.

## Jack Swagger

Oklahoma's favorite son, Jack Swagger has used his technical prowess in the ring to capture titles and championships in WWE. His ability is so impressive that announcer Michael Cole hired Jack to be his trainer for a big match at WrestleMania. Swagger's smarts and training helped Cole win several matches.

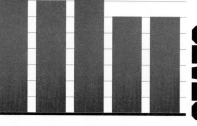

| 8 | 7 | 8 | 6 | 6 |
|---|---|---|---|---|
| Intensity | Strength | Speed | Courage | Brains |

**STATS**

| | |
|---|---|
| 6'6" | **Height** |
| 263 lbs. | **Weight** |
| Perry, Oklahoma | **From** |
| Ankle Lock; Gutwrench Power Bomb | **Signature Move** |
| World Heavyweight Champion; ECW Champion; Money in the Bank winner (2010) | **Career Highlights** |

**INFO**

# SIN CARA vs. TYLER REKS

Since bursting on the scene in 2011, Sin Cara has taken the WWE Universe by storm, garnering attention for his fast-paced offense and his colorful mask and ring attire. Tyler Reks is a little jealous of Sin Cara's popularity with the WWE fans. Reks would like to knock Sin Cara down a little so maybe the fans will notice him, too.

## Sin Cara

One of the most popular international Superstars of all time, Sin Cara made the WWE Universe fall in love with him from the moment he made his debut. He has a flashy style that is amazing to watch. And with an air of mystery about him, Sin Cara is a man who always entertains the fans when he gets in the ring.

**INFO**

| | |
|---|---|
| Height | 5'7" |
| Weight | 175 lbs. |
| From | Mexico City, Mexico |
| Signature Move | Springboard Moonsault; Hurricanrana |
| Career Highlights | Money in the Bank Participant |

**STATS**

| Intensity | Strength | Speed | Courage | Brains |
|---|---|---|---|---|
| 6 | 6 | 9 | 7 | 7 |

# THE SHOWDOWN:

As Sin Cara leaps into the ring from the floor, Tyler Reks doesn't give him a chance to play to the crowds. Tyler attacks Sin Cara immediately, doing anything he can to stop the Mexican sensation from using his vicious aerial attacks. Reks can't keep Sin Cara grounded for long, though. The "man with no face" climbs to the top rope and whips Reks down with a beautiful hurricanrana.

## Tyler Reks

With his dark soul and frightening appearance, Tyler Reks haunts the WWE. He sneaks around in a terrifying manner, plotting to strike his opponents when they least expect it. Reks often refers to himself as "T. Reks," and like the king of the dinosaurs, he loves devouring his opponents.

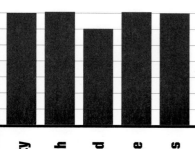

| 7 | 7 | 6 | 7 | 7 |
|---|---|---|---|---|
| Intensity | Strength | Speed | Courage | Brains |

**STATS**

| | |
|---|---|
| 6'3" | **Height** |
| 252 lbs. | **Weight** |
| Parts Unknown | **From** |
| Bruning Hammer DDT | **Signature Move** |
| 2010 Slammy Award for Most Menacing Haircut | **Career Highlights** |

**INFO**

# DREW MCINTYRE vs. HORNSWOGGLE

Everyone knows that Hornswoggle is a great mischief maker, but perhaps this time he's gone too far. After pulling a prank on Drew McIntyre, the little leprechaun earned the ire of the "Chosen One." WWE would never sanction a match between Hornswoggle and McIntyre, but that doesn't mean the two will never collide.

## Drew McIntyre

This Superstar thinks very highly of himself. From the time of his WWE debut as *SmackDown*'s "Chosen One," McIntyre has tried his best to steal the spotlight from whomever else it was shining on. He successfully captured the Intercontinental and Tag Team Championships, proving to the WWE Universe why he was chosen by Mr. McMahon to carry the WWE banner throughout the world.

## INFO

| | |
|---|---|
| Height | 6'5" |
| Weight | 256 lbs. |
| From | Ayre, Scotland |
| Signature Move | Future Shock |
| Career Highlights | Intercontinental Champion; WWE Tag Team Champion |

## STATS

| Intensity | Strength | Speed | Courage | Brains |
|---|---|---|---|---|
| 6 | 6 | 7 | 6 | 4 |

# THE SHOWDOWN:

As Hornswoggle playfully pulls pranks on the WWE Universe from the ring, his recent victim, Drew McIntyre, races to ringside. Hornswoggle won't be taken that easily, though. He races out of the ring and slides beneath it, seemingly disappearing. No one knows where he goes when he does that—he just disappears.

## Hornswoggle

Silly and playful, Hornswoggle brings smiles to the faces of the fans in the WWE Universe. He also annoys the WWE Superstars by constantly pulling pranks. Not much is known about Hornswoggle. It's believed that he has some special abilities to disappear and reappear unexpectedly. In any case, there's nothing predictable about WWE's favorite leprechaun.

## STATS

| | | | | |
|---|---|---|---|---|
| 3 | 2 | 2 | 3 | 7 |
| Intensity | Strength | Speed | Courage | Brains |

## INFO

| | |
|---|---|
| 4'4" | Height |
| 129 lbs. | Weight |
| Dublin, Ireland | From |
| Tadpole Splash | Signature Move |
| Cruiserweight Champion | Career Highlights |

# WILLIAM REGAL vs. JTG

William Regal is the epitome of class and grace. JTG is from the streets and doesn't care which fork one is supposed to use at dinner. This clash of lifestyles and heritages makes for great matches. And although they come from very different backgrounds, JTG and William Regal have similar in-ring styles. Both are brawlers—and they can't wait to brawl each other.

## William Regal

With the dignity to be expected from one of the Queen of England's most loyal supporters, William Regal has brought a level of refinement to the WWE. A strong and talented competitor in the ring, Regal has made his mark as an authority figure as well. He's been commissioner and general manager, making matches for the WWE Superstars. He's also a great teacher, having trained some of the best in the world, including Daniel Bryan.

## INFO

| | |
|---|---|
| Height | 6'2" |
| Weight | 240 lbs. |
| From | Blackpool, England |
| Signature Move | Regal Stretch |
| Career Highlights | Intercontinental Champion; World Tag Team Champion; European Champion; Hardcore Champion; WCW Television Champion; WWE Commissioner; Alliance Commissioner; Raw General Manager; King of the Ring (2008) |

## STATS

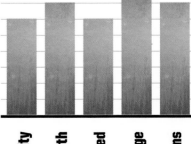

| | | | | |
|---|---|---|---|---|
| 6 | 7 | 6 | 9 | 7 |
| Intensity | Strength | Speed | Courage | Brains |

# THE SHOWDOWN:

It never takes long for either JTG or William Regal to start pummeling his opponent in the ring. When they face each other, it's almost as though they take turns striking. With Regal's 25 years of experience, he knows the best blows to throw, while JTG is always aware of a sneaky move to make.

## JTG

Growin' up in Brooklyn isn't the easiest thing in the world, but it made JTG tough. A former member of Cryme Tyme, JTG let the WWE Universe know there was only one thing he cared about: "Money, money, yeah, yeah!" With dollar signs in his eyes, JTG has battled some of the WWE's all-time greats. He knows that to get what you want, sometimes you have to just take it.

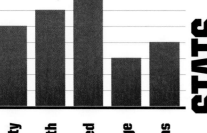

| | 5 | 6 | 7 | 3 | 4 |
|---|---|---|---|---|---|
| | Intensity | Strength | Speed | Courage | Brains |

**STATS**

| | |
|---|---|
| 6'1" | **Height** |
| 230 lbs. | **Weight** |
| Brooklyn, New York | **From** |
| Shout Out Neckbreaker | **Signature Move** |
| Former member of Cryme Tyme Tag Team | **Career Highlights** |

**INFO**

# EZEKIEL JACKSON vs. JINDER MAHAL

The Intercontinental Championship is one of the most prestigious titles in history, and Jinder Mahal wants it—bad. To get it, though, he has to defeat the gigantic and super strong Ezekiel Jackson. Jinder knows he's outsized, but he also knows he can outsmart big Zeke. But will that be enough? Or will Jackson's power overwhelm Jinder?

## Ezekiel Jackson

One of the most dominant WWE Superstars to ever compete in sports entertainment, Ezekiel Jackson grew up in a tough neighborhood where everyone had to fight to survive. But Jackson wouldn't have it any other way. He knows that the mean streets of Harlem gave him confidence and strength, which he has used to run over everyone in the WWE.

## INFO

| | |
|---|---|
| Height | 6'4" |
| Weight | 309 lbs. |
| From | Harlem, New York |
| Signature Move | Book of Ezekiel |
| Career Highlights | Intercontinental Champion; Final ECW Champion in history; Former member of The Corre |

## STATS

| Intensity | Strength | Speed | Courage | Brains |
|---|---|---|---|---|
| 8 | 9 | 5 | 6 | 7 |

# THE SHOWDOWN:

Although on paper this match looks like it will be all Ezekiel Jackson, Jinder Mahal has an ace up his sleeve: his protégé, the Great Kahli, is at ringside. Kahli's massive frame distracts Jackson, allowing Jinder to attack from behind. All the attack accomplishes, though, is making Jackson angrier. Jinder finds himself in trouble!

## Jinder Mahal

Throughout his life, things have come easy for Jinder Mahal. Living the life of royalty in India, Mahal never wanted for anything. When he came to the WWE, he saw that his fellow countryman, the Great Kahli, was struggling to stay in the main event picture. Mahal helped motivate Kahli to greatness, all the while knowing that Kahli had talents and size that would someday prove useful.

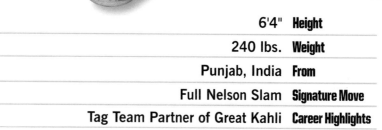

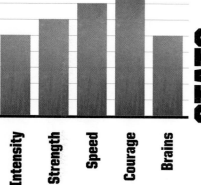

## STATS

| 5 | 6 | 7 | 8 | 5 |
|---|---|---|---|---|
| Intensity | Strength | Speed | Courage | Brains |

## INFO

| | |
|---|---|
| 6'4" | Height |
| 240 lbs. | Weight |
| Punjab, India | From |
| Full Nelson Slam | Signature Move |
| Tag Team Partner of Great Kahli | Career Highlights |

49

# ALICIA FOX vs. TAMINA

These two divas have everything to prove to the WWE Universe. Both are strong women who want to rise through the ranks in the Divas division and capture the WWE Divas Championship. To do that, though, each beautiful woman needs to get past the other.

## Alicia Fox

A former Divas Champion, Alicia Fox has spent her career in the WWE as the underdog. She's not the strongest Diva, or the most accomplished, but the WWE Universe knows that Alicia Fox is one of the hardest working. She studies ring technique and has become a talented threat to the other WWE Divas.

## INFO

| | |
|---|---|
| From | Ponte Vedra Beach, Florida |
| Signature Move | Scissor Kick |
| Career Highlights | Divas Champion |

## STATS

| Intensity | Strength | Speed | Courage | Brains |
|---|---|---|---|---|
| 4 | 4 | 7 | 5 | 6 |

# THE SHOWDOWN:

Alicia Fox's long, slender body makes it a little difficult to grab and lock on a hold. But Tamina's superior strength may give her the advantage she needs to keep Alicia from winning. Tamina proves this is possible by starting off the match with a big clothesline.

## Tamina

The daughter of WWE Hall of Fame inductee Jimmy "Superfly" Snuka, Tamina has followed in her father's footsteps by demonstrating that the sky's the limit for her in the WWE—literally! Like her famous flying father, Tamina is known for climbing to the top turnbuckle and diving off the top rope in a big splash—punishing her Diva opponents and racking up victories.

## STATS

| 8 | 6 | 5 | 5 | 5 |
|---|---|---|---|---|
| Intensity | Strength | Speed | Courage | Brains |

## INFO

| | |
|---|---|
| The Pacific Islands | From |
| Top Rope Splash | Signature Move |
| Former manager of the Uso brothers; Close friendship with Santino Marella | Career Highlights |

# EVE vs. MARYSE

Maryse is a "mean girl" who thinks she's prettier than the other WWE Divas. She brags about her boyfriends and their bank accounts, and treats the other Divas like they are less than she. Eve wants nothing more than to shut Maryse up. A much kinder person, Eve sticks up for the Divas and wants to teach Maryse that she's not better than the others.

## Eve

Eve began her WWE career by winning the 2007 WWE Diva Search. In the competition, she had to show the WWE Universe that she was confident, sexy, and athletic. Since winning the contest, Eve has continued to prove that she's just what she claimed to be: an incredible Diva. She even won the WWE Divas Championship!

**INFO**

| From | Denver, Colorado |
| --- | --- |
| Signature Move | Standing Moonsault |
| Career Highlights | WWE Diva Search Winner (2007); Divas Champion |

**STATS**

| | Intensity | Strength | Speed | Courage | Brains |
| --- | --- | --- | --- | --- | --- |
| | 5 | 3 | 6 | 8 | 7 |

# THE SHOWDOWN:

Maryse fights dirty—launching at Eve in her usual hair-pulling, eye-scratching routine. Eve, though, has some real ability, and she uses it to battle back. In a whirlwind, Eve throws Maryse out of the ring. Maryse desperately tries calling for a time-out, but there are no time-outs in sports entertainment.

## Maryse

With a sassy hand wave, Maryse tells the world that no one matters as much as she. The stunning French-Canadian Diva will accept only the most expensive gifts: diamonds, furs, and limousines. She is always on the lookout for a WWE Superstar who will buy her these pricey presents. The nonrich need not apply.

## STATS

| | | | | |
|---|---|---|---|---|
| 7 | 3 | 5 | 6 | 5 |

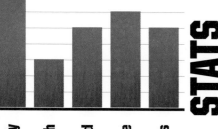

Intensity | Strength | Speed | Courage | Brains

## INFO

| | |
|---|---|
| Montreal, Quebec, Canada | From |
| French Kiss DDT | Signature Move |
| Divas Champion | Career Highlights |

# TRENT BARRETTA vs. TED DIBIASE

Trent Barretta and Ted DiBiase made their names as tag team Superstars. Since splitting from their respective tag teams, both have struggled to break into the main event scene on *SmackDown*. Each man is convinced that a victory over the other would be a huge step up the ladder of contenders to the World Heavyweight Championship.

## Trent Barretta

Trent Barretta debuted in the WWE as part of ECW's new talent initiative. He, along with his former tag team partner Caylen Croft, were popular in the now-defunct "Land of Extreme." Since ECW's end, Barretta has been competing on *SmackDown*— reminding the WWE Universe of his solid abilities in the ring.

## INFO

| | |
|---|---|
| Height | 6'1" |
| Weight | 230 lbs. |
| From | Akron, Ohio |
| Signature Move | Dudebuster DDT |
| Career Highlights | Former member of tag team the Dudebusters with Caylen Croft |

## STATS

| | | | | |
|---|---|---|---|---|
| 6 | 6 | 6 | 6 | 6 |
| Intensity | Strength | Speed | Courage | Brains |

# THE SHOWDOWN:

Ted DiBiase likes to complain to the WWE Universe about the injustices he's endured at the hands of *SmackDown* general manager Theodore Long. Trent Barretta uses one of these tirades to run to the ring, climb to the top rope, and land a spectacular flip-dive combination onto DiBiase.

## Ted DiBiase

The son of WWE Hall of Fame inductee "The Million Dollar Man," Ted DiBiase came into great wealth when a trust fund that had been set up for him became available. A third-generation Superstar, Ted has demonstrated that he's more than just a trust fund kid. He has good in-ring ability and has defeated many opponents.

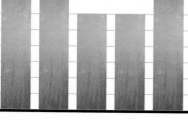

| 7 | 7 | 6 | 6 | 7 |
|---|---|---|---|---|
| Intensity | Strength | Speed | Courage | Brains |

**STATS**

| | |
|---|---|
| 6'3" | Height |
| 235 lbs. | Weight |
| West Palm Beach, Florida | From |
| Dream Street | Signature Move |
| World Tag Team Champion; Son of WWE Hall of Famer "The Million Dollar Man" Ted DiBiase, Sr.; Trained by WWE Hall of Famer Harley Race | Career Highlights |

**INFO**

# MICHAEL COLE vs. JERRY LAWLER

Tension at the *Monday Night Raw* announcer's table grew and grew until it came to a head. Play-by-play announcer Michael Cole insulted Jerry "The King" Lawler until Lawler could take no more. A WWE Hall of Famer, Lawler challenged Cole to a match. Cole was at first resistant, but when Lawler called him a coward, the match was on.

## Michael Cole

As the voice of WWE, Michael Cole became a trusted reporter, calling the action on *Monday Night Raw*, *Friday Night SmackDown*, and even on *WWE Superstars* and *WWE NXT*. But his ego got out of control, and the WWE Universe became annoyed with Cole's incessant self-promotion. Cole is still the lead announcer on many WWE programs, but he is no longer the trusted voice he once was.

## INFO

| | |
|---|---|
| Height | 5'9" |
| Weight | 168 lbs. |
| From | Amenia, New York |
| Signature Move | Not applicable |
| Career Highlights | Voice of the WWE; Multiple-time Slammy Award Winner |

## STATS

| Intensity | Strength | Speed | Courage | Brains |
|---|---|---|---|---|
| 7 | 3 | 4 | 8 | 3 |

# THE SHOWDOWN:

Michael Cole is a snake in the grass. Even before "The King" can get into the ring, Cole throws white powder in Lawler's eyes. Lawler wipes the powder from his face and charges Cole. Michael Cole has plenty of experience running away scared, and he puts that to good use—avoiding Lawler and his wrath in the ring.

## Jerry "The King" Lawler

For nearly four decades, Jerry "The King" Lawler has been involved in sports entertainment. He was a champion in a Memphis-based promotion and has been an announcer on *Monday Night Raw* for more than fifteen years. With all his accolades and accomplishments, one that "The King" holds highest is his induction into the WWE Hall of Fame.

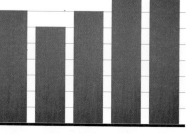

| | 7 | 6 | 7 | 8 | 9 |
|---|---|---|---|---|---|
| | Intensity | Strength | Speed | Courage | Brains |

**STATS**

| | INFO |
|---|---|
| 6'0" | **Height** |
| 243 lbs. | **Weight** |
| Memphis, Tennessee | **From** |
| Piledriver; Flying Fistdrop | **Signature Move** |
| AWA World Champion; WCCW Champion; Multiple-time regional champion in Memphis and Mid-South Wrestling; color commentator on Monday Night Raw; WWE Hall of Fame Inductee | **Career Highlights** |

# NATALYA vs. BETH PHOENIX

There is no question that Natalya and Beth Phoenix are the two strongest, toughest Divas in all the WWE. No one knows which of these two dynamite Divas is stronger. Although Beth and Natalya are friends, there's only one way to find out who is the true dominating Diva.

## Natalya

Natalya is a member of the legendary Hart family. Like the rest of her family, Natalya is known for having incredible technical ability in the ring. She is proud of the legacy passed on to her from grandfather, father, and uncles. The pink-and-black attack is determined to recapture the Divas Championship and keep it for a long time to come.

## INFO

| | |
|---|---|
| **From** | Calgary, Alberta, Canada |
| **Signature Move** | Sharpshooter |
| **Career Highlights** | Divas Champion; Daughter of WWE Legend Jim "The Anvil" Neidhart; Granddaughter of WWE Hall of Famer Stu Hart; Niece of WWE Hall of Famer Bret "Hit Man" Hart |

## STATS

| Intensity | Strength | Speed | Courage | Brains |
|---|---|---|---|---|
| 7 | 6 | 7 | 5 | 8 |

# THE SHOWDOWN:

As the two beautiful grapplers enter the ring, they begin with a long staredown from across the squared circle. Soon, though, they've locked up. Natalya gives Beth a shove, but Beth doesn't move. The "Glamazon" returns Natalya's shove, to similar results. Beth is certain she's stronger and tries to prove it with a big body slam.

## Beth Phoenix

Who says women can't be super strong and beautiful? Beth Phoenix, also known as "The Glamazon," is certainly both! After dominating the Diva division for several years, Beth made the leap to men's action, entering the Royal Rumble and competing against 39 male WWE Superstars for a chance to be in the main event at WrestleMania.

## STATS

| | | | | |
|---|---|---|---|---|
| 7 | 7 | 6 | 6 | 8 |
| Intensity | Strength | Speed | Courage | Brains |

## INFO

| | |
|---|---|
| Buffalo, New York | From |
| Glam Slam | Signature Move |
| Women's Champion | Career Highlights |

# THE BELLA TWINS vs. KELLY KELLY

Don't trust Brie and Nikki, The Bella Twins. The pretty sisters use their identical looks to fool their opponents, referees, and even the WWE Universe by switching places during matches. Doing so has led them to a lot of victories, something they hope will happen when they take on WWE Divas Champion Kelly Kelly.

## The Bella Twins

Brie and Nikki Bella, the mean-spirited twins from Arizona, like to team up to win matches and also to make fun of the other WWE Divas. Their favorite insult is to mock the physical appearance of their challengers. They know there's strength in numbers, so Brie and Nikki are always together. This makes them a difficult pair to defeat—in or out of the ring.

| INFO | |
|---|---|
| From | Scottsdale, Arizona |
| Signature Move | Twin Magic |
| Career Highlights | Divas Champion |

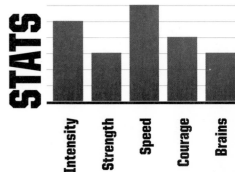

**STATS**

| | Intensity | Strength | Speed | Courage | Brains |
|---|---|---|---|---|---|
| | 5 | 3 | 6 | 4 | 3 |

# THE SHOWDOWN:

Like a pair of sharks about to feed, Brie and Nikki Bella circle Kelly Kelly in the ring. But Kelly Kelly is ready to take on whichever sister pounces first. It's Nikki! Or is it Brie? In either case, Kelly Kelly is taken to the mat hard by one of the Bella twins. It's a good thing Kelly Kelly is tough!

## Kelly Kelly

Kelly Kelly loves life. She's a sweet Diva who has spent her entire life dreaming of winning the WWE Divas Championship. She trained hard to be highly competitive in the ring and she has realized her championship dreams. As the Divas champion, Kelly Kelly takes on all comers, always ready to defend the title on *Raw* and *SmackDown*.

| 4 | 3 | 6 | 5 | 6 |
|---|---|---|---|---|

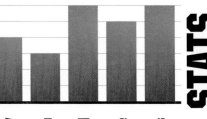

**Intensity** **Strength** **Speed** **Courage** **Brains**

**STATS**

| Jacksonville, Florida | From |
|---|---|
| Kelly Kick | Signature Move |
| Divas Champion | Career Highlights |

**INFO**

61

# BOOKER T vs. MATT STRIKER

Booker T and Matt Striker are color commentators on *Friday Night SmackDown*. Both have experience as WWE Superstars, which gives them insight into the matches and the personalities that compete on *SmackDown*. Both men have what it takes to be a great announcer, but who is the better wrestler?

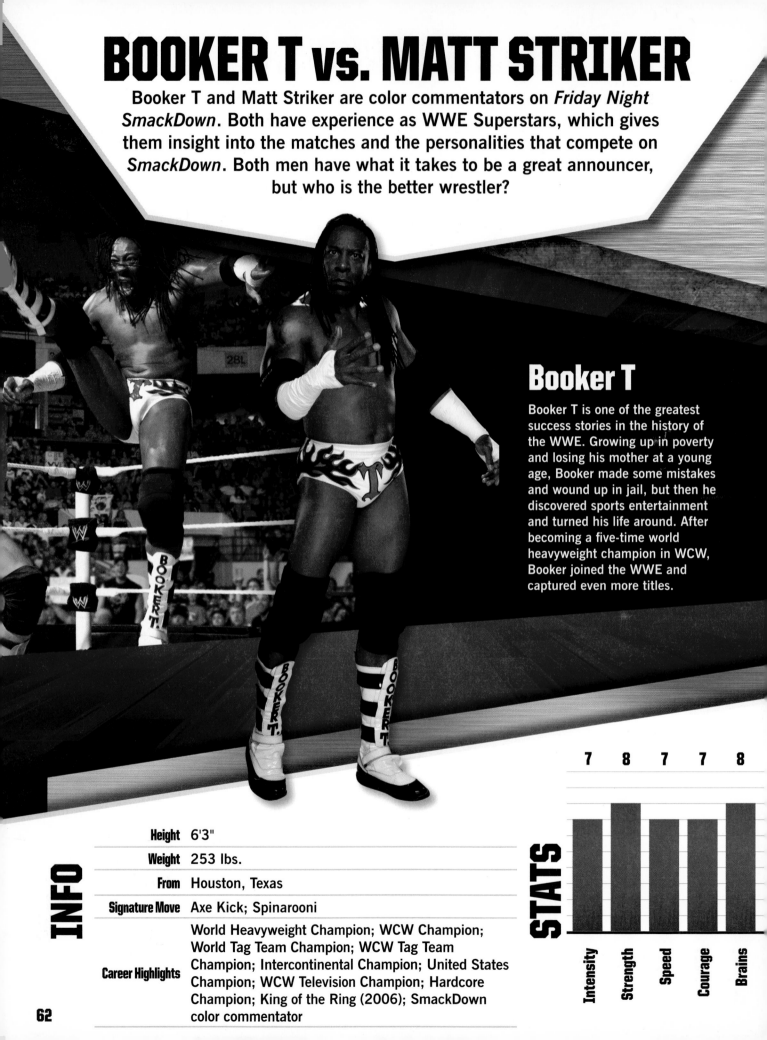

## Booker T

Booker T is one of the greatest success stories in the history of the WWE. Growing up in poverty and losing his mother at a young age, Booker made some mistakes and wound up in jail, but then he discovered sports entertainment and turned his life around. After becoming a five-time world heavyweight champion in WCW, Booker joined the WWE and captured even more titles.

## INFO

| | |
|---|---|
| Height | 6'3" |
| Weight | 253 lbs. |
| From | Houston, Texas |
| Signature Move | Axe Kick; Spinarooni |
| Career Highlights | World Heavyweight Champion; WCW Champion; World Tag Team Champion; WCW Tag Team Champion; Intercontinental Champion; United States Champion; WCW Television Champion; Hardcore Champion; King of the Ring (2006); SmackDown color commentator |

## STATS

| Intensity | Strength | Speed | Courage | Brains |
|---|---|---|---|---|
| 7 | 8 | 7 | 7 | 8 |

# THE SHOWDOWN:

Striker and Booker begin the match with friendly, smiling shoves. The friendliness fades quickly, however, and the two find themselves locked up in the center of the ring. Striker attempts to hit Booker with a clothesline, but Booker dodges and responds with a mighty spin kick, sending the former school teacher to the mat—hard!

## Matt Striker

Matt Striker is a smart man. A former school teacher in New York City, Striker has an encyclopedic knowledge of sports entertainment history and continues to teach the audience of *Friday Night SmackDown* about it. He occasionally gets back in the ring to compete but spends most of his time at the commentator's desk on Friday Nights.

## STATS

| Intensity | Strength | Speed | Courage | Brains |
|-----------|----------|-------|---------|--------|
| 4 | 6 | 6 | 9 | 7 |

## INFO

| | |
|---|---|
| 5'10" | Height |
| 224 lbs. | Weight |
| Bayside, New York | From |
| Not applicable | Signature Move |
| SmackDown commentator; Former ECW commentator; Former Host of NXT; Trained by WWE Hall of Famer Johnny Rodz | Career Highlights |

## 4–5. John Cena vs. CM Punk

WINNER: John Cena

After Punk fails to hit Cena with a GTS, Cena grabs Punk, lifts him on his shoulders, and hits him with the Attitude Adjustment for the victory.

## 6–7. Undertaker vs. Kane

WINNER: Undertaker

Kane is no match for the power of the creatures of the night, Undertaker's minions. Drawing strength from the creatures, Undertaker lifts Kane up and drives him to the mat with a tombstone.

## 8–9. Mark Henry vs. Big Show

WINNER: Mark Henry

Big Show had a fighting chance, but not after Mark Henry bashed Big Show's knee into the steel ring post. A World's Strongest Slam later, and Mark Henry is victorious.

## 10–11. Randy Orton vs. Christian

WINNER: Randy Orton

Christian had Randy Orton set up for the Killswitch, but Orton reversed it and out of nowhere hit an RKO on Christian, knocking Christian out cold.

## 12–13. The Miz vs. Alex Riley

WINNER: The Miz

The Miz hates to lose and will do anything to win, including hitting his opponent with the ringside bell. With Riley out, Miz steals the win.

## 14–15. John Morrison vs. R-Truth

WINNER: John Morrison

R-Truth may think there's a conspiracy against him, but tonight the only conspiracy was John Morrison, who used his trademark Starship Pain to pin R-Truth for a three count.

## 16–17. Dolph Ziggler vs. Kofi Kingston

WINNER: Dolph Ziggler

Kofi looked like he might stand a chance, but not after Vickie Guerrero distracted Kofi and the referee, allowing Ziggler to surprise Kofi from behind, pinning him 1-2-3.

## 18–19. Rey Mysterio vs. Alberto Del Rio

WINNER: Rey Mysterio

Del Rio grew more and more desperate as the match went on. So desperate, in fact, that he grabbed a steel chair from ringside. The referee saw Del Rio try to smash the chair on Mysterio and disqualified Del Rio, making Rey the winner.

## 20–21. Michael McGillicutty vs. Santino Marella

WINNER: Santino Marella

McGillicutty knocked Santino down and gloated to the crowd about it. This gave Santino a chance to use his dangerous Cobra Strike on McGillicutty, gaining the win.

## 22–23. Yoshi Tatsu vs. Tyson Kidd

WINNER: Tyson Kidd

Tyson Kidd is ruthless in the ring, and he used that excessive aggression, along with his technical ability, to lock Yoshi in a sharpshooter, making the Japanese sensation quit.

## 24–25. Zack Ryder vs. Curt Hawkins

WINNER: Zack Ryder

Zack Ryder made easy work of Curt Hawkins, showboating in front of the fans. Nobody likes a sore loser, but a sore winner is even worse!

## 26–27. Triple H vs. "Stone Cold" Steve Austin

WINNER: "Stone Cold" Steve Austin

It was a long back-and-forth battle, with many near-falls and close calls. But in the end, it was the Rattlesnake, "Stone Cold" Steve Austin, who surprised Triple H with a stone cold stunner to beat "The Game."

## 28–29. Brodus Clay vs. Johnny Curtis

WINNER: Brodus Clay

It was a match of brains vs. brawn, and in this case, the brawn won as Brodus Clay overpowered Johnny Curtis.

## 30–31. Mason Ryan vs. David Otunga

WINNER: Mason Ryan

Mason Ryan is just too powerful for Otunga; he comes away with the victory after driving his foe to the mat and getting the pin.

## 32–33. Jey Uso vs. Justin Gabriel

WINNER: Justin Gabriel

Gabriel trapped Uso on the mat in the corner. After climbing to the top rope, he hit his patented 450 splash, and there was nothing Jey could do.

## 34–35. Daniel Bryan vs. Cody Rhodes

WINNER: Daniel Bryan

Daniel Bryan locked in his inescapable LaBell lock, forcing Cody Rhodes to submit.

## 36–37. Heath Slater vs. Jimmy Uso

WINNER: Jimmy Uso

Heath Slater put up a valiant effort, but Jimmy Uso wasn't going to let the "One Man Rock Band" score a victory. Uso nailed Slater with a Samoan Drop for the victory.

## 38–39. Sheamus vs. Wade Barrett

WINNER: Sheamus

In another back-and-forth contest, Sheamus struggled to keep Barrett down on the mat. After a kick, it was a little easier—and it led to a big win!

## 40–41. Evan Bourne vs. Jack Swagger

WINNER: Jack Swagger

Swagger grounded Bourne by nearly breaking his ankle in the ankle lock. With Bourne unable to fly off the ropes, it became an easy win for Jack Swagger.

## 42–43. Sin Cara vs. Tyler Reks

WINNER: Sin Cara

As tough and terrifying as Tyler Reks is, it's Sin Cara's speed and high-flying moves that allow the mysterious masked superstar to get the victory.

## 44–45. Drew McIntyre vs. Hornswoggle

WINNER: Hornswoggle

Hornswoggle never reappeared after disappearing under the ring, so McIntyre was left wondering where Hornswoggle went. Since it wasn't a match, the Leprechaun won the battle.

## 46–47. William Regal vs. JTG

WINNER: William Regal

William Regal's experience proved to be too much for JTG to handle. Regal landed his powerful left punch and pinned the Brooklyn native.

## 48–49. Ezekiel Jackson vs. Jinder Mahal

WINNER: Ezekiel Jackson

Ezekiel Jackson was about to drop Jinder Mahal in a devastating slam when the Great Kahli got into the ring and attacked Jackson. The referee disqualified Jinder, but he and Kahli left Jackson lying in the ring as though he'd lost the match.

## 50–51. Alicia Fox vs. Tamina

WINNER: Alicia Fox

Although Tamina came out dominant, Alicia Fox's slender flexibility allowed her to twist free from every move Tamina tried. Alicia then surprised Tamina with a roll-up pin for the win.

## 52–53. Eve vs. Maryse

WINNER: Eve

Eve was on a mission, and she used her acrobatic talents to cut Maryse's legs out from under her. Maryse got fed up and walked out of the ring and out of the match, getting counted out and giving Eve the win.

## 54–55. Trent Barretta vs. Ted DiBiase

WINNER: Ted DiBiase

DiBiase recovered from Barretta's sneak attack and strapped on the Dream Street hold, sending Barretta down hard and scoring the pin.

## 56–57. Michael Cole vs. Jerry Lawler

WINNER: Jerry Lawler

When finally forced to face Lawler in the ring, Cole dropped to his knees and begged "The King" to stay away. Lawler responded with a couple of punches, and Cole was out cold immediately.

## 58–59. Natalya vs. Beth Phoenix

WINNER: Beth Phoenix

This match could have gone either way, as both Divas hit many moves and proved dominant. In the end, though, Beth Phoenix caught Natalya by surprise and hit her with a Glamazon Slam, ending the match.

## 60–61. The Bella Twins vs. Kelly Kelly

WINNER: Kelly Kelly

The Bella Twins tried cheating and double-teaming Kelly Kelly, but the champion was able to get a win by hitting a handspring elbow and pinning Nikki when Brie wasn't looking.

## 62–63. Booker T vs. Matt Striker

WINNER: Booker T

It came down to experience as Booker T capitalized on a mistake Striker made when he unsuccessfully tried to climb to the top rope. Alone in the ring after the match, Booker celebrated by doing a Spinarooni.